Covid-19 and the Law Relating to Food in the UK and Republic of Ireland – The Essential Guide

Ian Thomas is a dual-qualified specialist food lawyer practising in England and Wales (barrister 1993) and in Ireland (solicitor 2006).

He advises on a wide range of non-contentious and contentious EU and domestic food law matters including; food safety and hygiene, animal welfare (including at the time of killing), food information, health and nutrition claims, food supplements, borderline products, traceability, product withdrawals and recalls, official controls and enforcement powers.

Ian has substantial experience of advising or appearing in court to represent clients facing enforcement actions, appeals and prosecutions.

Ian is an elected Fellow of the Society of Food Hygiene and Technology (SOFHT).

He is a Contributing Lecturer to the PgC/PgD/MSc Food Regulatory Affairs course (University of Ulster/University College Dublin) and a guest lecturer on the Development of Food Law and Policy for the MSc Course in Applied Culinary Nutrition at Technological University Dublin (Tallaght).

Ian is a regular speaker at food law conferences and seminars and is a member of the Food Law Group, the Food Safety Professionals Association and is an affiliate member of the Institution of Occupational Safety and Health. He is also a member of the Certification Committee of Excellence Ireland Quality Association (the Q Mark).

He is a consultant with La Touche Training (Dublin) where he provides training on law, practice, procedure, evidence and courtroom skills.

Ian is the author of '*A Practical Guide to the Law Relating to Food*'.

"A very experienced and able operator... Very knowledgeable in food safety and hygiene." – Chambers and Partners

"A true food safety expert, he has a grasp of pitching his in-depth, technical knowledge in the most appropriate commercial context." – Legal 500

Covid-19 and the Law Relating to Food in the UK and Republic of Ireland – The Essential Guide

Ian Thomas LL.B (Hons), FSOFHT
Barrister-at-Law, 6 Pump Court, London
Solicitor, Ian Thomas Associates, Republic of Ireland

Law Brief Publishing

The information in this book was believed to be correct at the time of writing. All content is for information purposes only and is not intended as legal advice. No liability is accepted by either the publisher or author for any errors or omissions (whether negligent or not) that it may contain. Professional advice should always be obtained before applying any information to particular circumstances.

Published 2020 by Law Brief Publishing, an imprint of Law Brief Publishing Ltd
30 The Parks
Minehead
Somerset
TA24 8BT

www.lawbriefpublishing.com

Paperback: 978-1-913715-03-8

This book is dedicated to my family, with thanks for everything.

PREFACE

The law relating to food is now reasonably well established as a specialist area within the mainstream of legal theory and practice.

It is a vast subject bringing together science, regulation, law, academia and politics.

European food law, as applied in the EU member states, is flexible enough to react to threats to public health, consumer safety and to the free movement of compliant products.

The rules require that food is safe, produced in hygienic conditions and properly described. Where this fails, there are provisions aimed at removing non-compliant food from the market in order to protect consumers and take appropriate action against wrong-doers.

The system is tried and tested, albeit constantly developing to meet new challenges and remain fit for purpose. People generally know what is required, even if they do not always follow the rules to the letter.

Although measures are in place to protect the integrity of food production and supply, food professionals are used to dealing with situations where food is detrimental to consumers. This might be due to the presence of *Salmonella, Campylobacter, E. Coli, Listeria* or glass or other harmful physical contaminants, or allergens. These may harm consumers and may be fatal.

But now the entire food system faces a brand-new threat, from a brand-new virus which is not yet fully understood; Covid-19 (SARS-CoV-2).

There is little evidence that the virus is transmitted in food, although it may be transmitted on food or via surfaces that have been contaminated. The impact of Covid-19 has been very significant for the food supply chain and this has led to significant issues for consumers, food business operators and for regulators.

This book aims to identify some areas of food law and practice which have been or could be adversely affected by Covid-19. It provides some commentary on the problem and tentatively offers some thoughts that might be used to combat the threat and help food businesses re-open safely.

At the time of writing, early June 2020, the law and guidance on matters relating to Covid-19 is developing rapidly as governments strive to protect public health whilst enacting measures to avoid sustained and irreversible damage to business and the economy.

I have therefore tried to keep the book focused on general matters that can help the food industry come to grips with the problem and which I hope will be of benefit in the longer term as the effects of Covid-19 will be felt for many months, if not years.

I would like to thank everyone who has helped, supported and motivated me throughout my career both in the UK and Ireland; family, friends, food professionals (lawyers, scientists, academics, advisers and consultants), colleagues inside and outside the legal profession and, finally, to the barristers, clerks and support staff at 6 Pump Court.

I also wish to thank Tim Kevan and Garry Wright of Law Brief Publishing for allowing me the opportunity to write this book which I hope is informative and interesting as well as being enjoyable (in so far as a law book can be "enjoyable"!).

Any comments or observations made in the book are personal and do not necessarily reflect the view of others. All errors in the text are mine and mine alone.

Law, guidance, practice and commentary are based on the situation as at 12th June 2020

Ian Thomas
June 2020

CONTENTS

CHAPTER ONE
INTRODUCTION

"It is highly unlikely that people can contract Covid-19 from food or food packaging" (WHO/FAO Interim Guidance 7th April 2020).

If so, what is the point of a book on Covid-19 and the law relating to food?

The answer probably lies in the fact that there has been a major impact on food supply chains and on the ability of people to access food. This has led to significant challenges for food business operators and consumers alike.

The human cost of the pandemic, as well as the economic consequences cannot and should not be ignored or forgotten.

A significant number of people have become ill and many have died. The numbers continue to rise and are publicly shared by way of daily briefings. The human impact of Covid-19 must drive, educate, guide and inform how each of us takes responsibility for the protection of our own health and that of others.

What then are some of the implications of Covid-19 for food, food supply and food law? They are many and varied but the following are some that come to mind;

1) Closing borders;

2) Restrictions on travel and the movement of people and goods;

3) Closure of certain food businesses (temporary and permanent);

4) Limiting the number of customers and restricting the consumer experience (social/physical distancing; one customer out, one customer in, no browsing, use of face coverings and sanitisers for hands and trollies);

5) Threats to food safety, quality and hygiene;

6) Food security;

7) Food sustainability;

8) Consumer information (e.g. misrepresentation);

9) Consumers looking to food to prevent or cure Covid-19;

10) Potential for an increase in criminal activity;

11) Reduction in consumer trust;

12) Commercial, insurance and contractual issues;

13) Increase in e-commerce/distance selling;

14) Loss of employment (temporary and permanent);

15) Severe economic conditions (globally, regionally, nationally and locally);

This book cannot hope to cover all these issues and apologies are made in advance if your particular area of interest is not fully covered.

However, the intention is to provide information on a broad range of topics which it is hoped will be beneficial to all readers whether directly or indirectly.

The food sector must fully re-open as soon as possible but only if this can be done safely and in a way that renders the premises Covid-secure.

In this book I refer to businesses being Covid-secure and not Covid-safe or Covid-free as I believe this better reflects the reality.

Businesses must also be able to operate in a commercially viable way and the tension between health and economic factors is starting to take centre stage.

However, the priority must always be that safety comes before profit or any financial consideration. This means the safety of consumers, staff and food.

Two examples of the tensions created by Covid-19 are the physical distancing of 2 metres and the wearing of face masks or face covers.

Even as I write this book there are indications that that official guidance will reduce the distance to 1 metre in some settings and that there is increased pressure to wear face coverings when shopping or travelling on buses, trains, planes and the like.

Food businesses need to comply with their food, Covid-19 and health and safety obligations. In order to respond appropriately they need to understand the basic science behind Covid-19; what is it, how is it spread and how to protect against it.

The law, guidance and advice about Covid-19 and the global, regional, national, and local response to it is a rapidly developing area.

The re-opening of some food businesses is moving forward, and in some respects ahead of schedule, but there are still significant uncertainties about how they will operate in practice.

Some aspects of this book will probably be out of date by the time it is published or very soon after. For this reason, I have tried to approach the subject-matter from a general perspective having regard to basic principles. In this way it is hoped that the book remains relevant despite the ever-changing landscape.

The basic issues relating to Covid-19 raised in this book apply equally to the UK and Ireland, even if the law and guidance might differ in the detail.

A brief word about the UK. England, Wales, Northern Ireland and Scotland have their own national food laws and their responses to Covid-19 have not always been the same.

In an attempt to keep references to legal provisions to a minimum, I have not always cited the individual laws of each jurisdiction. Where necessary, for example to make a comparison with the law in Ireland, I have made reference to one or more UK laws.

Another reason for not dwelling too much on domestic law is that this book is intended to be a guide and not a textbook. In most cases a reference to the EU law is sufficient and for this purpose I treat the UK as part of the EU.

I have not touched on the implications of Covid-19 on Brexit and food law. That might be for another publication.

Finally, the book has at its core the follow principles of food law:

1) A high level of protection of human life and health;

2) The protection of consumers' interests, including fair practices in food trade, taking account of, where appropriate, the protection of animal health and welfare, plant health and the environment; and

3) The free movement in the Community of food and feed manufactured or marketed (which has been adversely affected by the

closure of many country borders although these restrictions are now easing).

This book may be read in conjunction with "A Practical Guide to the Law Relating to Food" also written by me and published by Law Brief Publishing.

CHAPTER TWO
WHAT IS COVID-19?

Coronavirus disease (Covid-19) is an infectious disease caused by a newly discovered coronavirus (SARS-CoV-2).

The true extent of the human cost of Covid-19 can be seen by the following figures published by the World Health Organisation on 11th June 2020.

Globally there have been 7,273,958 confirmed cases of Covid-19, 413,372 deaths and it has been detected in 216 countries, areas or territories.

In the UK the figures are; 290,147 confirmed cases with 41,128 deaths.

In Ireland the figures are 25,231 confirmed cases with 1,675 deaths.

Those numbers will continue to increase for a while and there are suggestions that the actual figures may be higher than quoted.

It is concerning to note that there have been recent examples of the resurgence of the virus and the re-introduction of lockdown measures.

Other coronaviruses include Middle East Respiratory Syndrome (MERS – present since September 2012)) and Severe Acute Respiratory Syndrome (SARS – recognised in February 2003). Covid-19 shares some similarities with them but there are also some differences to bear in mind.

As is now well publicised, the Covid-19 outbreak occurred in December 2019 in Wuhan, China. It rapidly spread across the globe leading to the World Health Organisation declaring it a pandemic on

11th March 2020. The impact of the virus continues to have a significant impact with no clear end in sight.

The most common symptoms of Covid-19 are well known; fever, dry cough, and tiredness. Other symptoms may include; aches and pains, nasal congestion, headache, conjunctivitis, sore throat, diarrhoea, loss of taste or smell or a rash on skin or discolouration of fingers or toes.

Some of these symptoms are also associated with "ordinary" colds and flu and even with seasonal conditions such as hay fever. This creates substantial challenges for food business operators and staff in trying to identify and manage incidents of Covid-19. Self-awareness, seeking appropriate medical advice and testing are important.

As food businesses start to re-open and staff return to interacting with themselves and customers, it is essential that owners, operators and their staff remain alert for early signs of the potential onset of Covid-19 and take all necessary precautions to prevent the spread of the virus. FBOs need to put in place contingency plans to manage a situation in which a member of staff has or might have the virus.

Covid-19 is primarily spread from person to person through small droplets expelled from the body when someone coughs, sneezes or speaks. This has led to the guidance around social, or perhaps more accurately, physical, distancing and the wearing of face coverings.

Guidance, in the UK, Ireland and globally has sometimes lacked clarity and has certainly lacked consistency of approach. Whilst this might be inevitable due to the uncertainties about the virus and country specific conditions, it has not helped businesses prepare and plan for the future.

Guidance recommended avoiding spending more than 15 minutes in close contact with other people.

Physical distancing and the wearing of face masks are two examples of the sometimes inconsistent and contradictory advice that has been given during this pandemic. I will return to those topics in a later chapter.

In addition to the person to person contact, droplets can land on surfaces such as handles, tables, chairs, handrails, cutlery and menus. If those objects are touched or handled then a person may become infected thus emphasising the importance of taking appropriate hygiene measures such as washing hands.

Coronaviruses, such as Covid-19, can survive for different lengths of time on different surfaces. This creates yet further confusion for businesses.

There is no set definitive period and research is ongoing but as a guide:

- Up to 5 days on plastic;
- Up to 4 days on glass, paper and wood;
- Up to 2 days on stainless steel

Some materials, such as copper, may be helpful in the fight against Covid-19 as coronaviruses might only survive on it for about 4 hours.

An understanding of the survival rates on different surfaces could help food business operators undertaken risks assessments and adapt their premises, equipment and materials to become Covid-secure.

At the time of writing, early June 2020, there is no vaccine for Covid-19. This means that we will all have to live with it and its consequences for many, many months to come. Even when a vaccine becomes widely available, we may never go back to pre-Covid days.

The lessons learned from adapting to Covid-19 should be used to inform better decision-making about how businesses operate and how they interact with consumers.

Some good might, or perhaps must, come from the substantial and lengthy interference with what we took for granted as being "normal" life.

CHAPTER THREE
THE LEGISLATIVE RESPONSE TO COVID-19

Despite the legislative response to Covid-19 to restrict movement, close premises and all the other changes to our daily lives, the human and financial consequences of the virus have been staggering.

The legal strategies to combat Covid-19 deployed in the UK and Ireland have been a combination of legislation, guidance, public awareness campaigns and daily briefings. It may be argued, at least during the initial stages of the crisis, that the responses have contributed, whether by accident or design, to instilling a sense of fear in the public as a tool to secure compliance with the public health messages.

Nevertheless, the response has required a concerted effort from everyone in all walks of life to abide by the rules or, put another way in the words of Simon Harris TD, the Irish Minister for Health, the need for a "collective sense of cop on".

Unfortunately, there has not always been full and complete cooperation and adherence to the rules and there are many examples of people deliberately spitting and coughing on others and acting beyond the spirit, if not the letter, of the law,

The legal response to Covid-19 led to a "lockdown" imposing stringent and unprecedented restrictions on freedoms which in the UK, Ireland and elsewhere we take, or at least took, for granted.

The way out of lockdown towards a return to pre-Covid days has been by way of phased relaxations of the restrictions and the creation of roadmaps to opening up the countries, industries and sectors.

It is not possible, or wise, to debate the rights and wrongs, or pros and cons, of the legislation at this stage of the pandemic. This may come later. The response has varied with each legislature striving to do its best for its citizens, its health services and its economy.

In this chapter, I will briefly set out some of the main Covid legislation in the UK and Ireland. However, this can be no more than an introduction or a guide as the legislation, particularly secondary legislation, is developing to meet changing circumstances.

Ireland

In Ireland, where there is a written Constitution, the Oireachtas (Irish Parliament) enacted the Health (Preservation and Protection and other Emergency Measures in the Public Interest) Act 2020 (Number 1 of 2020) which was signed into law on 20th March 2020 (but sections of the Act were "deemed to have come into operation" on earlier dates in March 2020).

The introductory statements to the Act make clear the exceptional nature of both the subject-matter and the severe restrictions on personal freedoms.

It is an Act:

> "... to make exceptional provision, in the public interest and having regard to the
>
> manifest and grave risk to human life and public health posed by the spread of the
>
> disease known as Covid-19 and in order to mitigate, where practicable, the effect of the spread of the disease known as Covid-19, to amend the Health Act 1947 to confer a power on the Minister for Health to make regulations prohibiting

> or restricting the holding of certain events or access to certain premises and to provide for enforcement measures; …"

The Act also notes that;

> " … an emergency has arisen of such character that it is necessary for compelling reasons of public interest and for the common good that extraordinary measures should be taken to deal with the immediate, exceptional and manifest risk to human life and public health posed by the spread of the disease known as Covid-19;"

The legislation acknowledges the risk from the virus and the action to minimise that risk by stating;

> "… the State is and its citizens are, in significant respects, highly exposed to the effect of the spread of the disease known as Covid-19;"
>
> and
>
> "… as a consequence, it is necessary for the State to take the measures in this Act to address the emergency and to defend and vindicate the rights of citizens to life and to bodily integrity;"

Section 10 inserted section 31A into the Health Act 1947 to enable the Minister of Health to make, "Regulations for preventing, limiting, minimising or slowing spread of Covid-19".

The Regulations empowered the Minister to restrict travel, require people to stay at home, prohibit events including those that "could reasonably be considered to pose a risk of infection with Covid-19 to persons attending the event" and "any other measures that the Minister considers necessary in order to prevent, limit, minimise or slow the spread of Covid-19".

The Minister must have regard to the "national emergency" arising from Covid-19, "the need to act expeditiously in order to prevent, limit, minimise or slow the spread of Covid-19" and "the advice of the Chief Medical Officer of the Department of Health" which has been very prominent during the pandemic.

Regulations introduced requirements such as not leaving your place of residence without reasonable excuse.

What amounts to a reasonable excuse is determined by the facts and circumstances existing at the time, but the Regulations provided one example namely that a person could leave their residence for specified purposes such as to go to an essential retail outlet for the purpose of obtaining certain items such as food beverages, medicinal products etc.

Legislation also made provision for the payment of financial support and allowances, "to mitigate the economic effects of the spread of the disease known as Covid-19".

The other main Irish Act is the Emergency Measures in the Public Interest (Covid-19) Act 2020 (Number 2 of 2020) which also recognised the risks of the virus and the restrictions necessary to fight it.

Section 2 defines the virus:

> "In this Act, "Covid-19" means a disease caused by infection with the virus SARS-CoV-2 and specified as an infectious disease in accordance with Regulation 6 of, and the Schedule to, the Infectious Diseases Regulations 1981 (S.I. No. 390 of 1981) or any variant of the disease so specified as an infectious disease in those Regulations."

As we enter June 2020, the Irish Roadmap to re-opening the country is well underway with a phased and gradual relaxation of restrictions. However, it is still not possible have a meal in a restaurant or a pint in a pub, or even get a haircut!

The UK

The UK statute is the Coronavirus Act 2020 (2020 Chapter 7) which is:

> "An Act to make provision in connection with coronavirus; and for connected purposes."

It became law on 25th March 2020.

Section 1, Meaning of "coronavirus" and related terminology states:

> "(1) In this Act—
>
> "coronavirus" means severe acute respiratory syndrome coronavirus 2 (SARS-CoV-2);
>
> "coronavirus disease" means Covid-19 (the official designation of the disease which can be caused by coronavirus).
>
> (2) A reference in this Act to infection or contamination, however expressed, is a reference to infection or contamination with coronavirus.
>
> (3) But a reference in this Act to persons infected by coronavirus, however expressed, does not (unless a contrary intention appears) include persons who have been infected but are clear of coronavirus (unless re-infected)."

The Act covers a wide range of topics such as the emergency registration of health professionals, temporary registration of social workers and the registration of deaths.

Sections 25 to 29, are under the heading of "food supply".

Section 25, Power to require information relating to food supply chains states:

> "(1) An appropriate authority may, subject as follows, require—
>
> (a) a person who is in a food supply chain, or
>
> (b) a person who is closely connected with a food supply chain, to provide relevant information to the authority.
>
> (2) In subsection (1) "relevant information" means information about matters which relate to an activity of the person, where the activity is connected with the food supply chain mentioned in that subsection."

The appropriate authorities are; the Secretary of State, the Scottish Ministers, the Welsh Ministers and the Department of Agriculture, Environment and Rural Affairs in Northern Ireland ("DAERA").

At the time of writing these provisions, and the supplemental provisions in Schedule 15 of the Act have not yet been enacted.

The timeline for the enactment of the Health Protection (Coronavirus, Restrictions) (England) Regulations 2020 (2020 No. 350) is interesting:

- Made at 1.00 p.m. on 26th March 2020

- Laid before Parliament at 2.30 p.m. on 26th March 2020

- Coming into force at 1.00 p.m. on 26th March 2020

The introductory text to the Regulations again highlights the severity of the problem:

> "The Secretary of State makes the following Regulations in exercise of the powers conferred by sections 45C (1), (3)(c), (4)(d), 45F (2) and 45P of the Public Health (Control of Disease) Act 1984 F1.
>
> These Regulations are made in response to the serious and imminent threat to public health which is posed by the incidence and spread of severe acute respiratory syndrome coronavirus 2 (SARS-CoV-2) in England.
>
> The Secretary of State considers that the restrictions and requirements imposed by these Regulations are proportionate to what they seek to achieve, which is a public health response to that threat.
>
> In accordance with section 45R of that Act the Secretary of State is of the opinion that, by reason of urgency, it is necessary to make this instrument without a draft having been laid before, and approved by a resolution of, each House of Parliament."

The Regulations revoked the (1) The Health Protection (Coronavirus, Business Closure) (England) Regulations 2020 which had come into force on 21st March 2020.

The Coronavirus Restrictions Regulations required that person responsible for carrying on a specified business including restaurants, cafes, bara and public houses must:

"(a) during the emergency period—

(i) close any premises, or part of the premises, in which food or drink are sold for consumption on those premises, and

(ii) cease selling food or drink for consumption on its premises; or

(b) if the business sells food or drink for consumption off the premises, cease selling food or drink for consumption on its premises during the emergency period.

These Regulations also stated that during the emergency period, no person may leave (subsequently "be outside of") the place where they are living without reasonable excuse.

The list of potential statutory reasonable excuses was similar to those contained in the Irish legislation and includes:

"the need—

(a) to obtain basic necessities, including food and medical supplies for those in the same household (including any pets or animals in the household) or for vulnerable persons …"

The list of statutory reasonable excuses was expanded by amending regulations.

Similar Regulations were enacted in Wales, Northern Ireland and Scotland.

Restrictions have been in place in the UK and Ireland for many weeks and will continue for many more weeks to come although there are clear signs that there is a dim light at the end of the tunnel.

CHAPTER FOUR
THE IMPACT OF COVID-19 ON FOOD SUPPLY SYSTEMS

There has been substantial interference with the food supply chain due to Covid-19.

The consequences of this include the distribution of unsafe food and other practices which adversely impact consumers' interests.

Food supply chains have become longer and more complex over many years. This was highlighted in connection with the incident in 2013 when horsemeat was detected in frozen burgers in Ireland. The fallout from that crisis was deep, significant and long-lasting. There have been alleged incidents of horsemeat adulteration in 2020 which has led to increased concerns about the safety and integrity of the food supply chain.

Interference with the food supply chain can also have a serious impact on food security and food sustainability.

The restrictions imposed globally, nationally and locally as a result of Covid-19 have had a detrimental impact on the interrelationships between producers, processors, suppliers, delivery, retail and consumers.

Perhaps the most obvious, and at the time most newsworthy, manifestation of consumer concern about supplies was in the early days of the pandemic in the UK and Ireland with the stockpiling, or panic buying, of foodstuffs and non-food items such as toilet rolls.

After a relatively short while, consumers realised that although there would be some interruption to supplies, the hard work and combined effort of stakeholders meant that essential, but not always first-choice, products would generally still be available.

Food security is more than whether or not we can get our favourite brand of baked beans in our chosen supermarket. It is about ensuring that all people, at all times, have physical, social, and economic access to sufficient, safe, and nutritious food that meets their food preferences and dietary needs for an active and healthy life.

This is an interesting and vital topic that goes way beyond the scope of this book, but now is a good time to review how peoples of the world are able to have access to the food they need to thrive, not just survive.

In the same way that governments across the world are introducing mobile applications to track and trace people who might have been exposed to Covid-19, similar technology can assist producers to source local markets for their foods. This not only makes food accessible to people in a way that avoids long and complex food chains, it helps to prevent otherwise safe, wholesome and nutritious food being wasted. But, as will be seen later, consumers looking to source local products, whether out of choice or necessity, might be exposed to non-compliant practices that leads to unsafe and misdescribed food which cannot be properly traced to its source.

Food banks and charities have also helped many thousands of people across the globe access food for free or at low prices. Although this book focusses on the impact of Covid-19 on food law, it must be remembered that many people are without work and hence without income. This financial insecurity may continue for a very long time and reduced spending capacity and capability will inevitably hinder the recovery of some "non-essential" parts of the food sector such as restaurants, cafés, hotels and bars with some of these closing for good.

Adequate financial support packages are essential to help businesses and individuals survive the pandemic.

Discussion of food security and waste leads to another discussion point around the impact of Covid-19; the sustainability of food systems during and after a pandemic.

Innovation to find alternative sources of healthy, safe and nutritious food sources is not new but the current crisis may provide the impetus for further progress in this area.

Recent developments around the use of insects as food sources in the EU could be one way forward, once the consumer has put to one side their perhaps understandable concerns about eating a "bug".

Although innovative solutions are necessary, it is crucial that the desire to find alternative food sources, does not compromise safety and hygiene and all necessary regulatory approval must be obtained (e.g. in accordance with the Novel Food Legislation).

As always in the area of risk profiling of foodstuffs, the work of the European Food Safety Authority (EFSA) is an invaluable source of information.

We can all play our part in relation to protecting food security and sustainability, although for a lot of people in the UK and Ireland, these are not significantly direct and pressing issues. For this we are thankful.

CHAPTER FIVE
THE CONSEQUENCES OF ANY INTERFERENCE WITH FOOD SUPPLY SYSTEMS

Interference with food supply systems can have a very direct and immediate effect on matters of food safety, authenticity, misdescription and food crime.

These activities are sometimes referred to as food fraud but despite the name, issues with the food supply chain as they affect consumers may occur without criminal deception or intent but due to negligence, incompetence or indifference.

In case the importance of food fraud is not sufficiently well known, the UK Department of Environment, Food and Rural Affairs (DEFRA) is currently (June 2020) undertaking a project which seeks to understand the global drivers of food fraud and to identify food fraud mitigation tools. Although the survey closed on 19th June 2020, the results and next steps are keenly awaited.

Irrespective of why the interference happened, the harmful effect on consumers will be the same, however the severity of the consequences for the person responsible will depend on their level of culpability.

There are undoubtedly pressures on some food businesses. These may be financial or might be caused by their inability to obtain their "usual" ingredients or products. In a broader sense the pressure might result from the general uncertainties created by Covid-19 and the long-term viability of their business.

As these pressures mount up it might be tempting to cut corners, use inappropriate or dangerous substitute ingredients, or simply not take sufficient care in the selection of suppliers, ingredients, products or in the way they conduct their food business.

These temptations must be avoided as they can have a profound impact on consumers, the business and the wider food industry.

With the impact of Covid-19 likely to be felt for a long time to come, it is almost inevitable that many food businesses will encounter problems with food or ingredients which they, purchase, produce or supply.

Food businesses must have a clear understanding of how, when and when food issues might occur. This will provide valuable information to help them risk assess the threats to their business and ultimately to identify and prevent, or minimise, risks to consumers.

There are many types of conduct that can have a serious impact on food businesses:

- Adulteration – the inclusion of an undeclared ingredient. This may be to reduce costs or to falsely improve quality
- Substitution – replacing a high price ingredient with a lower priced one
- Mislabelling – incorrectly describing a product to wrongly enhance its quality, origin, or safety or its price, or wrongly indicating that it has been produced in a particular way (e.g. organic)
- Counterfeiting – using labels or other methods to suggest that a product is genuine whereas it is fake. This can be particularly dangerous with fake alcohol products which contain methanol
- Unlawful processing – this might involve slaughtering animals in unlicensed premises

- False documents – used in connection with the supply of fake food

- Diversion – this might involve putting food destined for waste back into the human food chain

- Theft – food is stolen from a legitimate source and then sold into the human food chain. The food might have been stored or handled incorrectly leading to a risk of harm.

Diversion and theft are examples of the classic purchase of cheap, and potentially dangerous, food from the "back of a lorry". This activity should put most food business operators on notice of a "dodgy deal".

However, unlawful activity could also arise when meat prepared in an unapproved establishment is sold in what might appear to be legitimate circumstances. The problem is less obvious to unwitting food business operators and consumers, but the consequences could be equally severe.

The desire for putting financial considerations before safety can have significant consequences which include death of the consumer and imprisonment for the perpetrator.

Food business operators will have identified weaknesses in their own operations which could lead to problems and this should be re-visited in the light of additional threats caused by Covid-19.

Business owners will be familiar with HACCP (Hazard Analysis and Critical Control Point) for food safety but now might be an appropriate time to consider additional forms of protection:

- TACCP – Threat Assessment Critical Control Point – a process to defend against intentional contamination or to protect against malicious threats to food from sabotage, extortion or terrorism, and

- VACCP – Vulnerability Assessment Critical Control Point – a process to defend against dishonest conduct, such as economically motivated food fraud, and which has a detrimental impact on quality or authenticity of food

Unfortunately for legitimate food businesses, food crime can be extremely lucrative and the perpetrators will do everything they can to present their non-compliant food in the most authentic, legitimate and attractive way. Covid-19 not only increases the opportunities to perpetrate illegal activity but it creates a wider pool of potential targets.

As will be apparent from the above comments, the drivers for illegal action include financial troubles, pressures on the supply chain reducing the availability of ingredients and products. Long and complex supply chains can affect traceability.

A desire, or need, to shorten the supply chain can lead to a search for alternative supplies and suppliers closer to home. Of course, this is not necessarily wrong; it is after all one of the facets of innovation and change.

However, the search must be done properly, and food businesses must have regard to basic requirements around supplier audits and quality and safety checks of ingredients and products. Carrying out these tasks properly has been significantly hampered as a result of the restrictions.

When a new ingredient or product is brought into the food businesses the impact of this on food safety, quality and consumer information must be carefully assessed and managed appropriately.

Not being able to do the right thing "because of Covid-19" is not, nor should it be, an excuse for poor standards or for putting consumers at risk.

The impact of Covid-19 on the brewery and pub sectors shows the different types of consequences that can arise. Pubs are shut and consumer demand for beer is zero, or at least close to zero (there have been a number of pubs selling take away drinks). What then happens to all the beer that has been brewed but not sold?

Some has to be thrown away but this must be done carefully so as not to have any environmental damage. Some can be diverted for animal feed. These are obvious and visible.

What is less obvious is the societal impact of the closure of pubs which, in many areas, act as the hub of the community. Many pubs have safely diversified to meet the challenges and the need of local residents but there may be many unknown and currently unforeseen long-term consequences resulting from pub closures.

CHAPTER SIX
COVID-19, GENERAL FOOD LAW AND FOOD SAFETY

Food is not believed to be a route of direct transmission of the virus.

If food business operators build on their existing policies and procedures, they can go a long way to operating a safe, Covid-secure and compliant business.

Of course, one major stumbling block is knowing when certain food businesses will be permitted to re-open and how they will be required to operate in a Covid-secure way.

But again, innovation and diversification of the food offer have come to the fore with increased use of take-away, collection and delivery options by restaurants and even having pints delivered to your home!

Any operational changes must be managed carefully to comply with rules relating to safety, hygiene, food information and quality, and also to maintain the requirements of physical distancing, hand hygiene, cough and sneeze etiquette and use of face coverings.

The main EU law on food safety and general food law principles is Regulation (EC) 178/2002.

In Ireland the domestic law can be found in the European Communities (General Food Law) Regulations 2007 and in the European Communities (Food and Feed Hygiene) Regulations 2009.

Regard should also be had to the Food Safety Authority of Ireland Act 1998.

The law in the UK is contained in the Food Safety and Hygiene (England) Regulations 2013, The General Food Regulations 2004 (Wales and Scotland) and the Food Safety (Northern Ireland) Order 1991.

Regard should also be had to the Food Safety Act 1990 and the Food Safety (Scotland) Act 2015.

As with all EU Regulations, Regulation 178/2002 applies directly in each EU member state (for present purposes this includes the UK). Domestic legislation sets rules relating to enforcement and penalties for non-compliance.

As a useful starting point for considering the relationship between EU law and domestic law, it is worth recalling that terms and phrases used in the domestic law which appear in the EU law will have the meaning as in the relevant EU law.

So, for example, Regulation 2 (3) of the Food Safety and Hygiene (England) Regulations 2013 states:

> "Unless the context otherwise requires, any expression used both in these Regulations and in Regulation 178/2002 or the EU Hygiene Regulations has the meaning that it bears in Regulation 178/2002 or the EU Hygiene Regulations."

The "EU Hygiene Regulations are defined in Regulation 2 (1) as:

> "Regulation 852/2004, Regulation 853/2004, Regulation 854/2004, Regulation 2073/2005 and Regulation 2075/2005"

In Ireland the same principle applies. Regulation 2 (2) of the European Communities (General Food Law) Regulations 2007 states:

> "A word or expression which is used in these Regulations and which is also used in the EC Regulation has, unless the context otherwise requires, the same meaning in these Regulations as it has in the EC Regulation."

The term, "EC Regulation" as used in the Irish law is defined in Regulation 2 (1) and it:

> "means Regulation (EC) No. 178/2002 of the European Parliament and of the Council of 28 January 2002 laying down the general principles and requirements of food law, establishing the European Food Safety Authority and laying down procedures in matters of food safety"

Finding your way around any legislation is not always straightforward but by using the EU and domestic law in parallel, it is usually possible to find the meaning or definition for important legal terms and phrases.

This is not always the case. When we come to consider product withdrawals and recalls, recourse must be had to definitions contained in non-legislative materials.

In the remaining part of this chapter, I will set out some of the main food safety provisions. This is not intended to be, nor can it be, a complete and comprehensive review.

Food business operators must comply with all their obligations and should not ignore that basics of good food operations when focussing on the immediacy of Covid-19 requirements.

Regulation 178/2002 lays down the general principles and requirements of food law, establishes the European Food Safety Authority and also lays down procedures in matters of food safety.

This is sometimes referred to as "the General Food Law Regulation" or "GFLR".

Article 14.1 states that food shall not be placed on the market if it is unsafe.

Article 14 continues:

> "2. Food shall be deemed to be unsafe if it is considered to be:
>
> (a) injurious to health;
>
> (b) unfit for human consumption.
>
> 3. In determining whether any food is unsafe, regard shall be had:
>
> (a) to the normal conditions of use of the food by the consumer and at each stage of production, processing and distribution, and
>
> (b) to the information provided to the consumer, including information on the label, or other information generally available to the consumer concerning the avoidance of specific adverse health effects from a particular food or category of foods.

Injurious to health applies where a food has the potential to cause harm to human health whereas unfit for human consumption usually connotes a quality issue.

In the context of earlier discussions, food might be unsafe if a substitute ingredient has been introduced which could cause harm (e.g. an allergenic ingredient), or where the food is fake or a genuine product has been adulterated (product labelled as vodka but contains methanol) or where meat that has been deemed unfit for human consumption is diverted into the human food chain (meat produced in an unapproved establishment).

Article 18 of Regulation 178/2002 contains rules about traceability. The food business operator must be able to identify, and produce records if required, from whom they have been supplied with food and ingredients and also the businesses to which they have supplied their products.

This is defined as "the ability to trace and follow a food, feed, food-producing animal or substance intended to be, or expected to be incorporated into a food or feed, through all stages of production, processing and distribution" (Article 3 of Regulation 178/2002). This is commonly referred to as tracing one step back and one step forward.

Article 19 contains provisions applicable to the actions required where a food business operator "considers or has reason to believe that a food which it has imported, produced, processed, manufactured or distributed is not in compliance with the food safety requirements" or "if it considers or has reason to believe that a food which it has placed on the market may be injurious to human health." Proper traceability is crucial to be able to fulfil these obligations.

For the purposes of food law compliance, the food business operator has a fundamental role play. To the extent that the FBO is also an employer they will also have a crucial role to play in relation to Covid-19 and health and safety matters.

Article 3 of Regulation 178/2002 defines "food business operator" as:

> "the natural or legal persons responsible for ensuring that the requirements of food law are met within the food business under their control"

The food business operator bears primary responsibility for matters such as:

1) Food complying with food law (Article 17 of the GFLR);

2) Complying with traceability obligations (Article 18 of the GFLR);

3) Taking action to withdraw or recall non-compliant foods (Article 19 of the GFLR)

4) Compliance with hygiene requirements (Article 3 of Regulation 852/2004 – hygiene of foodstuffs – covered in a subsequent chapter);

5) Providing correct food information (Article 8 of Regulation 1169/2011 – covered in a subsequent chapter)

It is also important to have regard to the general statement about the protection of consumers' interests in Article 8 of Regulation 178/2002:

> "Food law shall aim at the protection of the interests of consumers and shall provide a basis for consumers to make informed choices in relation to the foods they consume. It shall aim at the prevention of:
>
> (a) fraudulent or deceptive practices;
>
> (b) the adulteration of food; and
>
> (c) any other practices which may mislead the consumer."

Regulation 178/2002 defines some important terms, some of which will be very familiar to food professional, including:

Food

Article 2 of GFLR defines food, sometimes referred to as foodstuff;

> "any substance or product, whether processed, partially processed or unprocessed, intended to be, or reasonably expected to be ingested by humans."

It includes:

> "drink, chewing gum and any substance, including water, intentionally incorporated into the food during its manufacture, preparation or treatment."

Certain items are excluded from this definition; feed, live animals (unless they are prepared for placing on the market for human consumption), plants prior to harvesting, medicinal products, cosmetics, tobacco and tobacco products, narcotic or psychotropic substances and residues and contaminants.

Other general terms are defined in Article 3;

Food law

> "means the laws, regulations and administrative provisions governing food in general, and food safety in particular, whether at Community or national level; it covers any stage of production, processing and distribution of food, and also of feed produced for, or fed to, food-producing animals"

Food business

> "means any undertaking, whether for profit or not and whether public or private, carrying out any of the activities related to any stage of production, processing and distribution of food"

Placing on the market

> "means the holding of food or feed for the purpose of sale, including offering for sale or any other form of transfer, whether free of charge or not, and the sale, distribution, and other forms of transfer themselves"

Although there is currently (early June 2020) no evidence to link transmission of Covid-19 through contaminated food, the following definitions are relevant for food businesses when undertaking risk assessments in the context of food and Covid-19:

Hazard

> "means a biological, chemical or physical agent in, or condition of, food or feed with the potential to cause an adverse health effect"

Risk

> "means a function of the probability of an adverse health effect and the severity of that effect, consequential to a hazard;

Risk analysis

> "means a process consisting of three interconnected components: risk assessment, risk management and risk communication"

Risk assessment

> "means a scientifically based process consisting of four steps: hazard identification, hazard characterisation, exposure assessment and risk characterisation"

Risk management

> "means the process, distinct from risk assessment, of weighing policy alternatives in consultation with interested parties, considering risk assessment and other legitimate factors, and, if need be, selecting appropriate prevention and control options

Risk communication

> "means the interactive exchange of information and opinions throughout the risk analysis process as regards hazards and risks, risk-related factors and risk perceptions, among risk assessors, risk managers, consumers, feed and food businesses, the academic community and other interested parties, including the explanation of risk"

There are clear parallels between the steps needed to comply with food safety law and also to comply with health and safety law and Covid-specific requirements. This should make the general approach to Covid-19 more manageable for food business operators.

CHAPTER SEVEN
COVID-19 AND FOOD HYGIENE

Food must be made in hygienic conditions to ensure that it is safe.

Food businesses know that good hygiene is important. The degree to which food premises are kept clean can be a visible sign of how well or badly the business is being operated.

Now that Covid-19 has elevated cleanliness of people, places, equipment and materials to an even higher status, food businesses can build on hygiene rules to become Covid-secure.

The main EU legislation can be found in Regulation (EC) No 852/2004 "on the hygiene of foodstuffs" (Regulation 852) which is supplemented by Regulation (EC) No 853/2004 "laying down specific hygiene rules for food of animal origin" (Regulation 853).

In Ireland the main laws are the European Communities (Hygiene of Foodstuffs) Regulations 2006 and the European Communities (Food and Feed Hygiene) Regulations 2009.

In the UK the law can be found in the Food Safety and Hygiene (England) Regulations 2013, the Food Hygiene (Wales) Regulations 2006, the Food Hygiene (Scotland) Regulations 2006 and The Food Hygiene Regulations (Northern Ireland) 2006.

Article 1 of Regulation 852/2004 confirms that "primary responsibility for food safety rests with the food business operator" (as defined above).

Article 2 of Regulation 852/2004 defines food hygiene, sometimes simply referred to as hygiene 'food hygiene', as "the measures and conditions necessary to control hazards and to ensure fitness for human consumption of a foodstuff taking into account its intended use".

Regulation 852/2004 requires food business operators to:

- Comply with general hygiene provisions/requirements;
    - in Annex I of that Regulation – if carrying out primary production (Article 4 (1))
    - in Annex II of that Regulation – if carrying out any stage of production, processing and distribution of food after primary production (Article 4 (2))
- As appropriate, adopt the specific hygiene measures (Article 4 (3);
    - compliance with microbiological criteria for foodstuffs;
    - procedures necessary to meet targets set to achieve the objectives of this Regulation;
    - compliance with temperature control requirements for foodstuffs;
    - maintenance of the cold chain;
    - sampling and analysis.
- Put in place, implement and maintain a permanent procedure or procedures based on the HACCP principles (Article 5);
- Any specific requirements provided for in Regulation (EC) No 853/2004 (Articles 4 (1) and (2))

Food business operators will already be operating a HACCP system or procedures based on those principles in respect of food safety.

Many practitioners in the UK and Ireland will be very familiar with the provisions in Annex I and Annex II of Regulation 852/2004. The latter in particular forms the basis of many food enforcement notices and prosecutions in both jurisdictions.

Those provisions of Annex II of particular relevance and importance in maintaining a food-compliant and a Covid-secure food business include the following:

- Food premises are to be kept clean and maintained in good repair and condition (Chapter 1, paragraph 1)

  Food premises that are untidy or what might be termed "dirty" make it very difficult to keep them clean properly and also reflects poorly on the Food Business Operator.

  (Care should be taken when using words like "dirty" in the context of food hygiene law as it does not necessarily mean that there is a hygiene risk).

- The layout, design, construction, siting and size of food premises are to:

  (a) permit adequate maintenance, cleaning and/or disinfection, avoid or minimise air-borne contamination, and provide adequate working space to allow for the hygienic performance of all operations; (Chapter 1 paragraph 2 (a))

  FBOs should review their food premises to ensure that all areas are capable of being easily, and frequently, cleaned and disinfected.

The question of providing sufficient work space is now inextricably linked to ensuring that staff keep the required physical distance from each other when in the kitchen and elsewhere within the food business.

As discussed above, coronaviruses can survive on surfaces for varying lengths of time.

In order to clean and disinfect surfaces properly, it may be necessary to increase the frequency of this process and obtain appropriate products such as Sodium Hypochlorite.

Care should be taken when selecting chemicals and technical data sheets should be checked.

Products should be viricidal not merely anti-bacterial.

All changes should be implemented properly including making revisions to written procedures on the use, handling and storage of these types of products and training staff on the correct and safe use of the chosen product (including the use of PPE where necessary).

Care should be taken when considering the use of spray or fogging type disinfectants within food premises as they can have adverse health consequences for staff.

- Where necessary, adequate changing facilities for personnel are to be provided (Chapter 1, paragraph 9).

  Again, this might be seen as having taken on greater significance in the era of Covid-19, particularly if staff have travelled on public transport.

- In rooms where food is prepared, treated or processed the design and layout are to permit good food hygiene practices, including protection against contamination between and during operations, in particular, surfaces (including surfaces of equipment) in areas where foods are handled and in particular those in contact with food are to be maintained in a sound condition and be easy to clean and, where necessary, to disinfect (Chapter II, paragraph 1).

  The above comments about coronaviruses surviving on surfaces and cleaning and disinfecting apply here.

- Adequate facilities are to be provided, where necessary, for the cleaning, disinfecting and storage of working utensils and equipment (Chapter II, paragraph 2).

  The above comments about coronaviruses surviving on surfaces and cleaning and disinfecting apply here.

- All articles, fittings and equipment with which food comes into contact are to be effectively cleaned and, where necessary, disinfected (Chapter V, paragraph 1).

  The above comments about coronaviruses surviving on surfaces and cleaning and disinfecting apply here.

- In relation to personal hygiene, Chapter VIII requires:

  1. Every person working in a food-handling area is to maintain a high degree of personal cleanliness and is to wear suitable, clean and, where necessary, protective clothing.

  2. No person suffering from, or being a carrier of a disease likely to be transmitted through food or afflicted, for

> example, with infected wounds, skin infections, sores or diarrhoea is to be permitted to handle food or enter any food-handling area in any capacity if there is any likelihood of direct or indirect contamination. Any person so affected and employed in a food business and who is likely to come into contact with food is to report immediately the illness or symptoms, and if possible, their causes, to the food business operator.

Although there is no evidence to show that food acts as a direct transmitter of Covid-19, it appears to be a virus that is readily transmitted between humans and as such it has the very real potential to be present in food business premises.

As mentioned above, the importance of regular handwashing/sanitisation must be reaffirmed to all staff and indeed to customers. This places an onus on the FBO to provide sufficient facilities to allow it to take place and to provide sufficient supervision to ensure it does take place.

Staff must be told and shown how to wash their hands properly. This may seem an obvious task and one which we were taught as children.

However, in recent weeks and months there has been much guidance and instruction, including in video form, on the correct way to wash hands properly.

Signs can be used to educate and remind staff of this very important requirement.

Recommendations in respect of handwashing note that hands should be washed for 20 seconds which equates to singing "Happy Birthday" twice.

But using simple techniques like singing "Happy Birthday" and the use of easy to read signs are very good and simple ways to keep the message relevant and fresh.

Listening to staff singing might show that they are hand-washing for the required length of time, but might not always be a pleasurable experience for colleagues and customers!

- The provisions applicable to foodstuffs in Chapter IX include:

1. A food business operator is not to accept raw materials or ingredients, other than live animals, or any other material used in processing products, if they are known to be, or might reasonably be expected to be, contaminated with parasites, pathogenic microorganisms or toxic, decomposed or foreign substances to such an extent that, even after the food business operator had hygienically applied normal sorting and/or preparatory or processing procedures, the final product would be unfit for human consumption.

3. At all stages of production, processing and distribution, food is to be protected against any contamination likely to render the food unfit for human consumption, injurious to health or contaminated in such a way that it would be unreasonable to expect it to be consumed in that state.

4. Adequate procedures are to be in place to control pests.

These provisions are well-known to most FBOs and, in my experience often feature in enforcement actions and prosecutions.

They also highlight some of the implications of Covid-19 referred to throughout this book.

The first provision goes to the heart of supplier auditing, particularly when sourcing alternative ingredients and products. If extra care is not taken the chances of having a contamination incident increases.

The second provision might appear to be of little relevance if it is highly unlikely that people can contact Covid-19 from food or food packaging. Nevertheless, there remains the possibility that if a member of staff is infected with the virus, whether or not symptomatic, and spreads it to food, particularly open ready to eat food, the virus could be passed to a customer.

In this example, the food could be an indirect transmission route, in the same way as if a customer touches a door handle or other surface (including packaging) contaminated with Covid-19.

If nothing more, the provision highlights the importance of avoiding contamination of food.

The provision relating to pests frequently appears in food enforcement cases.

There have been many reports of increased presence of pests, including rats, in premises that have been empty for some time.

When a food business is re-opening following a Covid shutdown, the FBO and its specialist contractors must pay particular attention to checking for pests, particularly in areas of the premises that might be hidden or not readily accessible.

There may be a pest infestation but it may not be obvious and this could cause significant problems for the business if it is not found and eradicated.

The perimeter of the building should be carefully checked for ingress points and they should be sealed without delay.

It would be very unfortunate if the business had to close soon after it had re-opened due to the presence of pests.

- Chapter X includes provisions applicable to the wrapping and packaging of foodstuffs

    1. Material used for wrapping and packaging are not to be a source of contamination.

    2. Wrapping materials are to be stored in such a manner that they are not exposed to a risk of contamination.

    As mentioned earlier, coronavirus can survive on packaging which could act as an indirect transmission route

Where food business such as restaurants, cafés and pubs have adapted by offering delivery services, they need to pay particular attention to the requirements relating to transport and maintaining food at the correct temperature.

Transport requirements are set out in Chapter IV of Annex II of Regulation 852/2004 and include:

- Conveyances and/or containers used for transporting foodstuffs are to be kept clean and maintained in good repair and condition to protect foodstuffs from contamination and are, where necessary, to be designed and constructed to permit adequate cleaning and/or disinfection.

- Receptacles in vehicles and/or containers are not to be used for transporting anything other than foodstuffs where this may result in contamination.

Of particular importance in relation to transporting foodstuffs is to clearly mark and segregate, where necessary, foods that contain any of the 14 specified allergens.

Whereas staff, and their supervisors, may have received adequate training in respect of their usual, pre-Covid, tasks, food business operators should ensure that they have been properly trained in their new roles.

As Covid-19 is spread person to person and potentially by touching contaminated surfaces or foodstuffs, staff need to understand the importance of, and practice, physical distancing and other measures such as face coverings and proper hand hygiene.

Training, implementation and supervision

Although the food philosophy is determined by the owners and operators of the business, its implementation is carried out by members of staff across all areas of the operation.

This might include corporate branding and style, customer awareness, corporate social responsibility and creating and maximising business opportunities.

When it comes to safety and hygiene, "… successful implementation of the procedures based on HACCP principles will require the full cooperation and commitment of food business employees. To this end employees should undergo training" (recital 13 of Regulation 852/2004).

The provisions around training are referred to elsewhere in Regulation 852/2004 particularly in Chapter XII of Annex II. Food handlers need to be "supervised and instructed and/or trained in food hygiene matters commensurate with their work activity" and those responsible for developing and maintaining HACCP procedures must have received adequate training.

Staff must also be fully and adequately trained in relation to Covid-19, just as with any other new hazards in the business, and also on the risk it presents to consumers, themselves and the business. This is made all the more difficult due to the changing and sometimes contradictory and confusing guidance that is available.

Registration and change of activities

Many food businesses in the hospitality sector have innovated and diversified to meet consumer demand and to keep their business afloat.

It should be recalled that food business operators must ensure that the competent authority always has up-to-date information on establishments, including by notifying any significant change in activities and any closure of an existing establishment (Article 6 of Regulation 852/2004).

Where a restaurant has moved to operating a take away the FBO should notify the relevant authority. Failure to do so is a criminal offence and if nothing else indicates a lack of knowledge of or commitment to complying with legal requirements.

CHAPTER EIGHT
FOOD INFORMATION, LABELLING AND CLAIMS

People are understandably apprehensive, if not fearful, of Covid-19.

Now, more than ever, they need to be confident that they can rely on the information they are given.

When people are fearful, they are more susceptible to being influenced and taken advantage of. This might be because of a desire to find a food that will help protect them against the virus.

This paves the way for unscrupulous operators and criminals to profit from this fear by making false claims about the composition or qualities of their products or the effect they may have on the human body.

It seems that many people have used the lockdown to take more exercise to improve their physical, and indeed mental, health. In some cases, this was one of the few opportunities they had for leaving home.

Proper nutrition and hydration are important for maintaining good health. We have seen an increase in cooking from scratch and one of the initial "panic-buy" items was yeast to satisfy the increase in making home-made bread.

It has not always been possible to maintain a proper level of nutrition due to a combination of many factors including lack of availability of and access to the right foods and ingredients and reduced income.

An internet search can readily provide information on the types of food that are good for the immune system. This can be helpful for consumers.

However, problems arise when food business operators seek to manipulate consumers into buying products with false, misleading or dangerous claims.

This is where the law relating to food information and claims sets a marker for what can, and what cannot, be said.

The rules relating to food information and nutrition and health claims are aimed at ensuring a high level of consumer protection. They must have regard to the differences in the knowledge and understanding of consumers and how statements and claims are perceived by them.

It is not my intention to refer to the law in detail but merely to identify some key legal provisions and the potential impact of them on Covid-19 issues.

Food Information

The primary EU food information law is Regulation (EU) No 1169/2011 on the provision of food information to consumers.

In the UK the domestic law can be found in The Food Information Regulations 2014, the Food Information (Wales) Regulations 2014, the Food Information (Northern Ireland) Regulations 2014 and the Food Information (Scotland) Regulations 2014.

In Ireland, the two main laws are the European Union (Provision of Food Information to Consumers) Regulations 2014 and the Health (Provision of Food Allergen Information to Consumers in respect of Non-Prepacked Food) Regulations 2014

Article 1 (2) of Regulation 1169/2011 (EUFIC) states:

> "This Regulation establishes the general principles, requirements and responsibilities governing food information, and

> in particular food labelling. It lays down the means to guarantee the right of consumers to information and procedures for the provision of food information, taking into account the need to provide sufficient flexibility to respond to future developments and new information requirements." (my emphasis)

Key definitions contained in Article 2 are:

> *Food information* – information concerning a food and made available to the final consumer by means of a label, other accompanying material, or any other means including modern technology tools or verbal communication;
>
> *Food information law* – the Union provisions governing the food information, and in particular labelling, including rules of a general nature applicable to all foods in particular circumstances or to certain categories of foods and rules which apply only to specific foods;
>
> *Mandatory food information* – the particulars that are required to be provided to the final consumer by Union provisions
>
> *Label* – any tag, brand, mark, pictorial or other descriptive matter, written, printed, stencilled, marked, embossed or impressed on, or attached to the packaging or container of food;
>
> *Labelling* – any words, particulars, trademarks, brand name, pictorial matter or symbol relating to a food and placed on any packaging, document, notice, label, ring or collar accompanying or referring to such food;

In seeking to protect consumers' interests, food information law provides a basis for consumers to make informed choices and to make safe use of food with regard to health, economic, environmental, social and ethical considerations (Article 3 (1) EUFIC).

Article 7 of EUFIC sets out some general, but very important, principles which apply to food information which also apply to advertising and the way in which foods are presented;

- Food information must be accurate, clear and easy to understand for the consumer.
- Food information must not be misleading, particularly:
    1) As to the characteristics of the food and, in particular, as to its nature, identity, properties, composition, quantity, durability, country of origin or place of provenance, method of manufacture or production;
    2) By attributing to the food effects or properties which it does not possess;
    3) By suggesting that the food possesses special characteristics when in fact all similar foods possess such characteristics, in particular by specifically emphasising the presence or absence of certain ingredients and/or nutrients;
    4) By suggesting, by means of the appearance, the description or pictorial representations, the presence of a particular food or an ingredient, while in reality a component naturally present or an ingredient normally used in that food has been substituted with a different component or a different ingredient.
- Food information must not attribute to any food the property of preventing, treating or curing a human disease nor refer to such

properties (and note that this prohibition specifically applies to food supplements – Article 6 of Directive 2002/46/EC).

This last provision is very relevant where foods are advertised as of claim to be capable of curing or preventing Covid-19.

Reference should also be made to similar provisions in Article 16 of Regulation 178/2002:

> "Without prejudice to more specific provisions of food law, the labelling, advertising and presentation of food or feed, including their shape, appearance or packaging, the packaging materials used, the manner in which they are arranged and the setting in which they are displayed, and the information which is made available about them through whatever medium, shall not mislead consumers."

Article 8 of EUFIC sets out the principles for identifying the food business operator that is responsible for providing food information. The primary responsibility lies with the FBO under whose name or business name the food is marketed. If that person is not established in the EU then responsibility falls on the importer. Article 8 imposes obligations in others in the food chain such as retailers.

The list of mandatory particulars to be indicated are set out in Article 9 (1):

(a) the name of the food;

(b) the list of ingredients;

(c) any ingredient or processing aid listed in Annex II or derived from a substance or product listed in Annex II causing allergies or intolerances used in the manufacture or preparation of a food and still present in the finished product, even if in an altered form;

(d) the quantity of certain ingredients or categories of ingredients;

(e) the net quantity of the food;

(f) the date of minimum durability or the 'use by' date;

(g) any special storage conditions and/or conditions of use;

(h) the name or business name and address of the food business operator referred to in Article 8(1);

(i) the country of origin or place of provenance where provided for in Article 26;

(j) instructions for use where it would be difficult to make appropriate use of the food in the absence of such instructions;

(k) with respect to beverages containing more than 1,2 % by volume of alcohol, the actual alcoholic strength by volume;

(l) a nutrition declaration.

Reference should also be made to Article 10 and Annex III for additional mandatory requirements such as foods packed in a protective atmosphere and foods containing sweeteners and having a high caffeine content.

Attention should be drawn to the requirements to label the 14 specified allergen ingredients (see Annex II of EUFIC):

1. Cereals containing gluten, namely: wheat (such as spelt and khorasan wheat), rye, barley, oats or their hybridised strains, and products thereof, except:

    (a) wheat-based glucose syrups including dextrose;

(b) wheat-based maltodextrins;

(c) glucose syrups based on barley;

(d) cereals used for making alcoholic distillates including ethyl alcohol of agricultural origin;

2. Crustaceans and products thereof;

3. Eggs and products thereof;

4. Fish and products thereof, except:

(a) fish gelatine used as carrier for vitamin or carotenoid preparations;

(b) fish gelatine or Isinglass used as fining agent in beer and wine;

5. Peanuts and products thereof;

6. Soybeans and products thereof, except:

(a) fully refined soybean oil and fat;

(b) natural mixed tocopherols (E306), natural D-alpha tocopherol, natural D- alpha tocopherol acetate, and natural D-alpha tocopherol succinate from soybean sources;

(c) vegetable oils derived phytosterols and phytosterol esters from soybean sources;

(d) plant stanol ester produced from vegetable oil sterols from soybean sources;

7. Milk and products thereof (including lactose), except:

   (a) whey used for making alcoholic distillates including ethyl alcohol of agricultural origin;

   (b) lactitol;

8. Nuts, namely: almonds (Amygdalus communis L.), hazelnuts (Corylus avellana), walnuts (Juglans regia), cashews (Anacardium occidentale), pecan nuts (Carya illinoinensis (Wangenh.) K. Koch), Brazil nuts (Bertholletia excelsa), pistachio nuts (Pistacia vera), macadamia or Queensland nuts (Macadamia ternifolia), and products thereof, except for nuts used for making alcoholic distillates including ethyl alcohol of agricultural origin;

9. Celery and products thereof;

10. Mustard and products thereof;

11. Sesame seeds and products thereof;

12. Sulphur dioxide and sulphites at concentrations of more than 10 mg/kg or 10 mg/litre in terms of the total SO 2 which are to be calculated for products as proposed ready for consumption or as reconstituted according to the instructions of the manufacturers;

13. Lupin and products thereof;

14. Molluscs and products thereof.

It has already been noted that due to supply chain issues and pressures on food business operators arising from Covid-19, there exists the potential for adulteration and ingredient substitution. Where this includes using one of the above ingredients which is not properly identified, this can have fatal consequences for consumers.

The date of minimum durability is the date until which the food retains its specific properties when properly stored.

This is particularly relevant to issues of food waste and changes in shopping habits including fewer trips to the shops. It could also be relevant where businesses with a stock of unsold product attempt to sell food, possibly quite cheaply, that has passed its use by date and has become unsafe.

There continue to be public health awareness campaigns to explain the difference between a best before date and a use by date.

There are many publicly available resources which explain the difference and the following is taken from the website of ***safefood***, a food and nutrition research, education and communication body operating on the island of Ireland:

> "The "**use-by**" date tells you when the food will become unsafe to eat.
>
> You should not eat the food after this date has passed.
>
> The use-by date is only valid as long as the food is stored properly, and the packaging is sealed. For instance, cooked meats should be stored in a fridge at 5° Celsius or less.
>
> The food label will also tell you how long the food will stay safe after opening the packaging. Normally, you should eat it within two or three days.
>
> The 'best before' date tells us when the quality of the food will begin to get worse.
>
> This means that the food might begin to lose its flavour and texture after that date, but it would still be safe to eat.

> The "**best-before**" date will only be valid if you store the food according to the instructions on the label. "Store in a cool dry place" or "Keep in the fridge once opened" are common storage instructions."

Where a date has been applied to a food it should only be changed, usually by way of extending the date, by the producer or manufacturer. This might be considered where, due to Covid-19, foods have been stockpiling due to the inability to sell it along the food chain. Great care should be taken whenever this considered and as always, consumer safety must be the primary consideration.

Many food businesses in the hospitality sector have started to provide a takeaway, collection or delivery service. This requires careful planning to ensure that the business is compliant with all food law requirements and the quality of their food remains high (this is not always the case).

One key issue to be aware of is the information requirements applicable to distance selling of food (Article 14 of Regulation 1169/2011). This is particularly important in that allergen information, a potential food safety issue, must be provided before purchase and again at the moment of delivery.

Rules in respect of non-prepacked food are contained in Article 44 EUFIC and in domestic legislation.

Nutrition and health claims made on food

The main EU law is Regulation (EC) No 1924/2006 on nutrition and health claims made on foods (NHCR)

The UK laws can be found in the Nutrition and Health Claims (England) Regulations 2007 with equivalent regulations in Wales, Northern Ireland and Scotland.

In Ireland the relevant law is the European Communities (Nutrition and Health Claims made on Food) Regulations 2014.

Regulation 1924/2006 (NHCR) applies to:

> "nutrition and health claims made in commercial communications, whether in the labelling, presentation or advertising of foods to be delivered as such to the final consumer." (Article 1 (2))

Article 2 (1) of the NHCR includes the following definitions:

> Claim – any message or representation, which is not mandatory under Community or national legislation, including pictorial, graphic or symbolic representation, in any form, which states, suggests or implies that a food has particular characteristics
>
> Nutrition claim – any claim which states, suggests or implies that a food has particular beneficial nutritional properties due to:
>
> (a) the energy (calorific value) it
>
> (i) provides;
>
> (ii) provides at a reduced or increased rate; or
>
> (iii) does not provide; and/or
>
> (b) the nutrients or other substances it
>
> (i) contains;
>
> (ii) contains in reduced or increased proportions; or
>
> (iii) does not contain;

Health claim – any claim that states, suggests or implies that a relationship exists between a food category, a food or one of its constituents and health

The law only applies to nutrition and health claims made in a commercial communication which is where the food business operator advertises their foods in a way that is designed to promote, directly or indirectly, those foods. It does not apply to activities such as public health guidelines.

The NHCR sets out the criteria for making nutrition and health claims. In essence a nutrition claim (such as low energy, contains vitamin C or fat-free) may only be used if they appear in the Annex to the NHCR and all applicable conditions are complied with.

Health claims (such as calcium is needed for the maintenance of normal bones or vitamin C contributes to the reduction of tiredness and fatigue) may only be used if they are authorised and any conditions of use are complied with.

Advertising standards

When food business operators are considering making statements or claims about their products, regard should also be had, where appropriate, to advertising codes issued by the Advertising Standards Authority of Ireland (ASAI) and the Advertising Standards Authority (ASA-UK). Although these Codes do not generally apply to packages, wrappers and labels, they do apply to advertisements in newspapers, magazines, brochures and the like.

The Codes reiterate some of the general principles set out above by stating that marketing communications must not mislead and must be legal, decent, honest and truthful and they must comply with the spirit and the letter of the Codes.

The Codes contain sections dealing specifically with food and nutrition and health claims and their rulings on complaints can be instructive.

There is additional guidance issued by the Food Standards Agency and the Food Safety of Ireland on the use of various marketing claims such as fresh, natural, pure, traditional etc.

Covid-19 issues

Mandatory food information requires a list of ingredients. If the food business operator has many pre-printed labels containing the list of usual, pre-Covid ingredients, but has had to change an ingredient what should the FBO do in order to avoid becoming non-compliant?

The strict answer is that the product, via its label, will be non-compliant if it lists an ingredient which is not in the product or does not list an ingredient that is in the revised Covid-era product.

The issues that need to be considered include:

1) What is the "new" ingredient. How does it affect the quality of the product and, much more importantly how does it affect its safety?

2) Is there a risk that the new product might contain one of the 14 specified allergens that must be declared? If so then this must not be used unless it is properly described on the label or in other food information;

3) What is the source of the new ingredient? Has the FBO undertaken sufficiently robust due diligence to ensure that the new supplier has done its own due diligence and has proper procedures in place?

4) Is the change of ingredient a short, temporary change or is it a permanent change? If the latter, then steps must be taken to prepare new, compliant labels.

If the non-compliant product is detected then there is a possibility that the FBO might be obliged to withdraw or recall the product from the market.

If the non-compliance does not affect the safety of the food then it might be possible to negotiate with the regulator to allow the non-compliant product to be sold through while the discrepancy is resolved (reverting to the original ingredient, preparing new compliant labels etc.).

The US FDA has considered a temporary amendment to food labelling laws to allow FBOs to make minor changes to ingredients that do not affect the safety of the food without having to revise the product label.

Some FBOs might see an opportunity to misdescribe or misinform consumers about the quality, composition or function of the food in question. This may be well-intentioned, due to ignorance or intentionally for profit.

They may seek to promote that a food is particularly safe, and safer than other foods, or that their product will prevent, or cure, Covid-19. They might suggest that the food, or one of its ingredients is being tested as a possible cure for Covid-19.

Such statements are likely to fall foul of the rules where the claims are unsubstantiated, false, misleading and/or make medicinal claims.

CHAPTER NINE
WITHDRAWALS, RECALLS AND NOTIFICATIONS

The chances of a food business being embroiled in a food incident will increase as a result of Covid-19.

Therefore, withdrawal and recall policies and procedures should be reviewed as a matter of urgency to ensure they are still fit for purpose, having regard to changes brought about by the crisis.

Some elements of the pre-Covid crisis management plan may no longer be applicable and some of the people involved in the crisis management team may no longer be available due to termination, redundancy or furlough (that new word in our vocabulary). The team might include personnel from; senior management with decision-making powers, finance, quality, engineering, technical, food science, HR, administration, public affairs/communication and legal.

Food incidents, withdrawals and recalls must not be thought of as something separate and outside of the FBO's basic processes and procedures. The ability to deal quickly, efficiently and effectively with food incidents must be an integral part of any food safety management system.

Taking time away from operational matters might seem unnecessary and an additional "burden" but a good crisis management plan and team are "worth their weight in gold" when called upon to protect consumers and the business.

It may be necessary to revise the plan and engage new people to manage it.

This must be done before it is needed as trying to revise a plan and seeking volunteers during the crisis itself will be very difficult.

It should be remembered that almost any FBO can become embroiled in a food incident whether or not they have caused it. All FBOs have an obligation to communicate and cooperate in order to achieve the ultimate goal; to protect the health of consumers.

It should also be recalled that even the best run businesses can inadvertently become involved in a food incident.

Before moving on, it may be worth explaining what we mean when we say; food incident, withdrawal and recall.

While they are not defined in food law, we use these terms in the following way:

Food incident

any event where, based on the information available, there are concerns about actual or suspected threats to the safety of food that could require intervention to protect consumers' interests.

Withdrawal

the process by which unsafe food is removed from the supply chain, where unsafe food has not yet reached the consumer

Recall

the process by which unsafe food is removed from the supply chain and consumers are advised to take appropriate action, for example to return or dispose of the unsafe food

These definitions are taken from the FSA publication, "Guidance on Food Traceability, Withdrawal and Recalls within the UK Food Industry" and I believe they are equally valid in Ireland.

As will be appreciated by most food business operators, time is of the essence during a food incident and the focus must be on taking immediate steps to protect consumers and the business which cannot be done effectively if the plan is inadequate and there is no one to operate it.

The plan of action for a food crisis contains two equally important phases; proactive and reactive.

The proactive phase is divided into two parts. Firstly, the FBO puts in place all the steps necessary to prevent an incident occurring; setting up and maintaining the usual food safety management systems – HACCP, training, cleaning, maintenance, supplier audits, internal checks and the like. Potential issues arising from Covid-19 require separate consideration. Secondly, the FBO creates a plan to deal with a food incident such as setting up a crisis management team and a crisis management plan that will be put into operation at the first mention of a food incident.

Traceability and the proper management of the supply chain are crucial aspects of this stage.

The reactive phase kicks in when the food incident happens. The crisis management team will be ready, willing and available to ensure the plan operates smoothly, efficiently and effectively in order to minimise the disruption and potential damage to the business.

The legal obligations on food business when faced with a food incident are set out in Article 19 of the General Food Law Regulation (178/2002).

Although references to legal provisions in this book have been kept to a minimum, it may be helpful to set out Regulation 19 in full:

> "Responsibilities for food: food business operators
>
> 1. If a food business operator considers or has reason to believe that a food which it has imported, produced, processed, manufactured or distributed is not in compliance with the food safety requirements, it shall immediately initiate procedures to withdraw the food in question from the market where the food has left the immediate control of that initial food business operator and inform the competent authorities thereof. Where the product may have reached the consumer, the operator shall effectively and accurately inform the consumers of the reason for its withdrawal, and if necessary, recall from consumers products already supplied to them when other measures are not sufficient to achieve a high level of health protection.
>
> 2. A food business operator responsible for retail or distribution activities which do not affect the packaging, labelling, safety or integrity of the food shall, within the limits of its respective activities, initiate procedures to withdraw from the market products not in compliance with the food-safety requirements and shall participate in contributing to the safety of the food by passing on relevant information necessary to trace a food, cooperating in the action taken by producers, processors, manufacturers and/or the competent authorities.
>
> 3. A food business operator shall immediately inform the competent authorities if it considers or has reason to believe that a food which it has placed on the

market may be injurious to human health. Operators shall inform the competent authorities of the action taken to prevent risks to the final consumer and shall not prevent or discourage any person from cooperating, in accordance with national law and legal practice, with the competent authorities, where this may prevent, reduce or eliminate a risk arising from a food.

4. Food business operators shall collaborate with the competent authorities on action taken to avoid or reduce risks posed by a food which they supply or have supplied."

The "food safety requirements" means the obligation not to place food on the market if it is unsafe (Article 14 of Regulation 178/2002).

A detailed review of the intricacies of a food withdrawal or recall is not possible here, but what are the implications of Covid-19 on the conduct of such a process?

1) <u>Receiving the initial notification of a problem</u>

If a business is not fully operational or is operating with reduced staff numbers, the normal channels of communication into the business may not be available. This can slow down the business's ability to respond appropriately to an external report of a problem (e.g. from a consumer or a regulator).

Even the usual internal channels may be interrupted.

The business must therefore put in place a mechanism by which any complaints of a problem with its products will be dealt with.

2) Reacting to the problem

The food business must identify the issue and the cause, as well as trying to establish how much product might be affected and where it is located.

The current limitations and restrictions could slow down the process.

If the affected product is still within the immediate control of the initial food business the Regulation 19 obligations are not engaged.

3) Investigating the problem

Having identified the hazard, the food business will conduct a risk assessment to identify the measures than need to be taken.

Again, this may not be as straightforward as it would have been pre-Covid-19.

The necessary people may not be on site, external laboratories may need to be engaged, samples may need to be taken and tested.

4) The crisis management team meeting

This may require some or all of the team communicating remotely. It is probably correct to say that people are becoming more used to communicating in that way but extra care needs to be taken to ensure that decision-making, note taking and the recording of decisions, and checking they have been properly implemented are all done correctly, agreed and signed off.

5) Making the decision

This is not always straightforward.

Four main issues fall to be considered; what do we need to do, when do we need to do it, how do we need to do it and who do we need tell.

The essence of the Regulation 19 provisions is the protection of consumer health and all decisions should be taken with this in mind.

However, an inevitable additional consideration is how to minimise the adverse impact on the business, but this should always be a secondary consideration.

6) Ongoing developments

Managing a rapidly developing food incident is not always easy at the best of times but it is essential that the team is kept up to date about what is happening to make sure that actions are not missed.

If the crisis management plan has a checklist of actions then this will assist to keep track of what has been done and what needs to be done.

If not then care need to be taken to ensure that simple things are not missed

7) Managing suppliers and customers

Identification of suppliers and customers (not including the final consumer) will be made easier where the business has developed a good traceability system.

Notifying them, by contacting the appropriate person, may not be as straightforward due to staff turnover, restricted working, furloughed staff and changes with that other business.

In the ordinary course of events, the FBO making the notification will check that the notified person has received the communication (e.g. the e-mail or telephone message).

This process now might not be as straightforward and may take longer than usual with the consequence that warning others of a potentially hazardous food on the market takes longer, thus increasing the potential risk to consumers (and to the business).

Even where the correct person has received notification, their response may be slower than would usually be expected due to restrictions within their own business.

How can the business be sure that its request for action has been understood and carried out correctly and that all the affected product has been retrieved and dealt with properly?

8) Communicating with the regulator

This should be one process that is not significantly affected by Covid-19.

The FSAI, local authorities and other regulators, have incident report forms available on-line. As will be seen from the text of Regulation 19, the FBO needs to tell the regulator what has happened and in the event that a food "may be injurious to human health", the FBO shall "inform the competent authorities of the action taken to prevent risks to the final consumer".

The on-line forms are a useful guide as to what information the regulator expects to receive.

As always, an informal notification to the regulator to notify them of the problem can be considered even if this is in the early stages when the business is still gathering information and making an assessment of the situation.

The regulator wants to know what has occurred, what are the risks to health and what the business is doing to prevent this. They want a plan of action and Covid-19 should not unduly delay this.

9) Communicating with consumers

Depending on the circumstances, the FBO will have to tell consumers what has happened, what the business is doing and, more importantly, what the consumer should do.

The consumer notice remains a vital tool in sharing the message but if trips to the shops are becoming less frequent during Covid-19, the retail point-of-sale notice, while remaining important, may need to be supplemented with other actions.

The regulators publicise food incidents and they are often made available on social media.

10) Recovering the affected product

Affected product may need to be returned to the retailer and then to the producer/manufacturer.

This process needs to be properly managed during a time when resources may be stretched.

The "usual" Covid precautions should be taken having regard to the potential for the survival of the virus on packaging.

11) <u>Finalising and evaluating the actions taken</u>

When is a food incident over?

Is it when all affected product has been accounted for or when there is no longer a risk to consumers? The regulator might have a say in this. However finality is measured, the FBO needs to be able to decide when that time has been reached.

Once the incident is over, the FBO must evaluate how it handled the situation. Again, this might be done at a time when limited resources are focussed on the business becoming and staying Covid-secure.

However tempting it is to delay the review or evaluation, this should not be done as the potential for further withdrawals or recalls remains a significant possibility.

The business should be very self-critical in how its own resources handled the situation. Did the plan, or Covid-revised plan, work effectively. If not, why not?

Were the staff able to do what needed to be done? Was their ability to do the job hampered by Covid restrictions and if so how and why?

What needs to be done to make sure any mistakes are not repeated during a subsequent incident?

How efficient and effective was the business able to communicate with its suppliers, customers, regulators and consumers?

Ultimately, the question is what lessons can we learn and the answer is to make the necessary changes immediately.

Much of what was done pre-Covid was done by remote means but there was always the option of physically taking action. Going to a supplier or to a retailer to check on how things were being handled was not a problem. That fallback position, or additional method of checking how the situation is being handled, is not as readily available as before.

Food business operators should take time to review how they will respond to a food incident whether it is of their own making or attributable to a deliberate or unintentional act by others.

A plan that is not fit for purpose is of no value. Trying to make it fit for purpose while simultaneously dealing with a real food incident will not be easy and will create additional, and unwelcome risks for consumers and for the business.

CHAPTER TEN
NON-COMPLIANCE AND LEGAL PROCEEDINGS

The restrictions on movement have had an impact on audits, inspections and enforcement.

This may have had and may continue to have an impact on levels of compliance and this may be reflected in increased numbers of enforcement actions and legal proceedings.

Food business operators will be doing all they can to ensure that they operate in a manner consistent with food law obligations and will proactively make any changes to procedures that are necessary.

It must be recalled that FBOs and employers have significant legal obligations.

It must also be remembered that employees are also required to act in a proper, responsible and compliant manner, once they have been fully trained and provided with the appropriate equipment and materials (including where applicable, PPE) to perform their roles safely.

During the pandemic it has not been as easy for food business operators to obtain the services of their regular consultants and auditors to help keep them on the right path.

Of course, it has been possible to continue to obtain advice and training using remote methods but that is not always as good as a face to face meeting. In addition, it is more difficult to show someone how to use equipment in a kitchen unless the trainer and trainee are physically in the same place.

The restrictions have also meant that physical inspections by regulators have been affected.

However, as we will see shortly, this has not prevented regulators from taking action where necessary to protect public health.

However, as the economy opens up and businesses start to return to some form of commercial activity, food business operators will need to be conscious of the Covid-focused workplace inspections by health and safety inspectors from the Health and Safety Executive, local authorities and the Health and Safety Authority.

Even if there is a reduction in the number of "official" inspectors, food businesses will be under intense scrutiny by an army of "unofficial" inspectors from the general public and this should be an additional incentive for all businesses to be remain vigilant and compliant at all times.

If a regulator, such as an environmental health practitioner, inspects a food premises during the current crisis, and in the immediate aftermath, how will they respond to any non-compliances?

The short answer is that this is likely to depend on the nature and extent of the non-compliance and its actual or potential impact on consumer health. The attitude and approach of the food business operator and their staff, along with the measures taken to become compliant will be highly relevant.

It is to be hoped, if not to be expected, that food regulators will, in the first instance follow the hierarchy of enforcement and fall back on their obligations to provide advice and guidance to assist food businesses that are clearly trying to do their best in a difficult situation.

Regulators, and where necessary business operators, should have full regard to enforcement policies and other documents designed to guide authorities in their approach to non-compliance.

In Ireland, the Food Safety Authority of Ireland, publishes monthly enforcement reports which include the number of premises closed down or that have received other enforcement orders during that month. This list also publicised in various media outlets so public awareness is high and could have a significant detrimental impact on the businesses concerned.

Although only three orders were served in May 2020, they are particularly relevant in that they show the types of activity that might be related to issues within the supply chain.

The reasons for the orders included:

- The establishment was operating without registration or approval (it was involved in the storage, processing and national distribution of meat). This meant that official controls were not taking place and it was not possible to verify compliance with food law;
- An absence of appropriate HACCP based food safety management systems, a failure to identify food safety hazards;
- No monitoring procedures to ensure the maintenance of the cold chain including transportation by an unregistered food business operator without refrigerated or temperature-controlled transport facilities;
- Failure to declare allergenic ingredients and raw meat labelling not labelled clearly with consumer instructions to cook thoroughly before eating;
- Unlabelled meats which could not be reliably traced back to the establishment of origin; and
- Products not labelled with a use by date.

The facts relied on to serve an enforcement notice may form the basis of a criminal prosecution as can non-compliance with the notice itself.

However, the regulator needs to give careful thought to how it seeks to achieve compliance and how it can "force" the food business into a situation in which there is no longer a risk to consumer health.

Regulators' actions should be proportionate, reasonable and necessary.

It may be that using emergency powers to close particularly dangerous premises achieves that aim. In order to be allowed to re-open, the business will need to clean up its act, both literally and metaphorically.

The use of enforcement notices might be sufficient although in most cases the FBO has the power to challenge the closure or the enforcement notice either internally or to a court or tribunal. Whether this is the right thing to do will depend on the particular circumstances.

For businesses that have clearly sustained significant financial decline, the regulator must give very careful consideration to whether it is necessary to take non-compliance matters further and commence criminal prosecutions.

Although the precise mechanics of the commencement and prosecution of criminal offences is different within the UK jurisdictions and in Ireland, there are some general issues to be considered.

A criminal prosecution should only be commenced if there is sufficient reliable, credible and admissible evidence to provide a realistic, or reasonable, prospect of conviction. If there is not then there is no prosecution.

The second limb of the test is that a prosecution should only be commenced if it is in the public interest. The impact of Covid-19 on the business could be a relevant factor. Advisers should therefore liaise with food clients to ascertain the full extent of the interference to business activities caused by the virus. In an appropriate case, this might be sufficient to persuade a regulator that a prosecution is not necessary.

There is a public interest in prosecuting serious, lengthy or repeated non-compliances, particularly where consumers have been put at risk.

The financial circumstances of every convicted company or individual, are relevant when the court comes to impose sentence.

In England and Wales, the judge is bound to follow the Definitive Guideline for food safety and hygiene offences. For an organisation, the judge has to identify the relevant sentencing table for the offender, which is based on its turnover, usually assessed having regard to its accounts for the preceding three years. The range of sentences in the guideline goes up to £3 million.

As a criminal case can take many months to come to court, by the time the judge is carrying out the sentencing exercise, the food business may have a significantly reduced turnover and little, if any profit which is attributable to Covid-19. In some cases, the business will have made a loss or may have had to close.

The judge will have to consider the impact of that changed financial position when she or he decides on the appropriate penalty. Where submissions are to be made about the adverse consequences of Covid-19, it seems to me that the FBO's representatives should prepare a full financial position statement, using accountants where necessary, in order to assist the judge to come to a fair and balanced decision.

In some cases, the business might have experienced a temporary blip in its fortunes from which it has recovered by the time of the hearing. In other cases, there may be ongoing or longer lasting financial implications.

If legal proceedings have already been commenced against the food business the chances are that there will be a virtual hearing conducted by telephone or via a video conferencing service. Courts and lawyers in the UK and Ireland are becoming more familiar with hearings being conducted remotely. Nevertheless, many court cases involving alleged breaches of food legislation are being adjourned until such time that a physical court hearing can take place.

Dealing with a hearing remotely is very different to a hearing in court before the judge. It requires adapting the normal skill set used by lawyers so that they can continue to put forward the best case on behalf of their client.

The fundamentals of a remote hearing are much the same as a physical hearing. Preparation and communication with client, other lawyers and the court remain vital. A thorough understanding of the case and the arguments to be made are always key starting points.

However, with a remote hearing there is a shift in the balance between written and oral presentation with greater emphasis being placed on the former.

The written submissions must present the facts in a clear, logical way so that the judge has a good understanding of the issues in advance of the hearing.

This allows for more concise, structured and focused advocacy on the day of the remote hearing. As we have all probably experienced over the last few months, it is much more difficult speaking to someone via a computer screen than it is in person.

When addressing a judge remotely, it can be difficult to pick up a sense of which arguments are gaining traction and which ones are not.

It is very difficult to conduct a hearing when your own team is not in the same place. This emphasises the importance of pre-hearing consultations with the client and with any experts.

Remote hearings will never truly replicate the solemnity of the hearing room.

Giving evidence is stressful at the best of times. Doing so via a computer, possibly from your own home, can be very difficult, particularly for lay clients who are unfamiliar with the process.

From a defendant's perspective, it can seem surreal having justice dispensed while they are sitting in their living room or kitchen!

Everyone participating in the court process should be given the opportunity to become familiar with giving evidence and addressing the court by remote means. It may be necessary for there to be frequent breaks, so that lawyers and clients can discuss the case. This can interrupt the flow of proceedings.

When lawyers and clients do need to have discussions during the remote hearing this must be done in a way that is safe and secure. Maintaining lawyer-client confidentially is crucial.

The court service is doing all it can to try and keep things ticking over, and we must all work with it. There will be teething problems and only time will tell whether issues emerge from the current and future conduct of remote hearings that generate challenges, not necessarily to the decision, but to the way in which the decision was reached.

CHAPTER ELEVEN
OPERATING A FOOD BUSINESS IN THE ERA OF COVID-19

In some respects this chapter could, and some might say should, provide a full list of all the most up to date and relevant information necessary for a food business operator to operate their food business safely and in a Covid-secure way; this chapter should therefore be the panacea for all Covid-19 ills.

Although it was tempting, I resisted.

This is partly because each food business is different having its own issues, problems and solutions. A chapter in a book like this cannot ever hope to be the answer for everyone.

There is an abundance of information available about how to operate a business on a Covid-secure way in addition to the vast array of guidance on food related matters.

There are return to work protocols, return to work checklists, return to work questionnaires and all manner of published material to help the business operators and their staff.

Ultimately, food business operators must use their own knowledge of their businesses combined with the assistance of their food consultants and advisers, and, hopefully the regulators, to adapt to operating in the new world in which we find ourselves.

Instead, I will list a few general issues for consideration that might give "food for thought" (some are mentioned elsewhere in this book and they are not in any particular order).

1) A Covid-19 return to work protocol,

2) Using a relevant return to work checklist;

3) Reminders about Covid-19; what is it, how it is spread and how can this be minimised or prevented;

4) What are the hygiene protocols; hand washing and cough and sneeze etiquette;

5) What is the guidance on physical distancing and how to adapt premises – one-way systems, signage, not having people waiting near each other, screens between staff and customers having booking times and not having walk-ins;

6) Use of face coverings – will they be mandatory in some premises such as restaurants, will staff be required to wear one, will customers be required to wear one?

7) Menus – single use disposable ones, laminated ones that can be cleaned after each customer, more use of menu boards – will the provision of allergen information be adversely affected by any changes?

8) Toilets – how to maintain proper hygiene standards and maintain physical distancing;

9) Not having live music – singing may increase the spread of the virus and possibly no DJs.

The FBO will have to adapt the basics of food law compliance with operating in accordance with Covid-19 laws and guidance. They will have to expect greater scrutiny by consumers who are now very familiar with what they expect to see to make them safe and secure.

Covid-19 has led to many changes including behavioural changes. Some of these are based on fact, some on misinformation and some on deliberate fake news. It is sometimes not easy to sort the "wheat from the chaff".

There is a saying; "Not only must Justice be done; it must also be seen to be done".

This may now be read as; "Not only must hygiene be done; it must be seen to be done".

At one level, consumers will expect to see visible and overt examples of the food business operator and their staff taking the necessary precautions. This might be physical distance signage, openly and deliberately being seen to wash hands and regularly cleaning and disinfecting surfaces. The second and third of these should be second nature in a food business but the operator might need to ensure that they are being seen to be done as a form of consumer reassurance.

It is therefore not enough to simply provide the facilities to make businesses Covid-secure. Staff must be very open and visible in following the appropriate hygiene requirements and checking to see that their colleagues and everyone else is doing the same.

Customers probably take for granted that the FBO is providing safe food made in hygienic conditions and think no more about it. It is "behind the scenes" and out of sight.

The expectation with Covid-19 is that the required safety measures are upfront; they must be overt and visible to staff and consumers. There is nowhere to hide. If the consumer expects to see something and it is not there, or is not visible, then this could be a source of trouble for the business (resulting in complaints and/or referrals to the regulators).

In order to maintain public trust, FBOs must not only provide the right visual appearance, they must also take measures to ensure that their procedures are being followed by staff and by consumers.

This might mean more frequent training, closer supervision and disciplinary action being taken when transgressions occur.

But how do staff deal with customers who refuse to physically distant or otherwise follow the rules? Should they be asked to leave the premises and if they refuse what happens next. It is hoped that the vast majority of people understand the need for Covid rules, even though they might not agree with them.

But there will always be the odd person who will deliberately not comply with requests to take appropriate action. We have seen examples of people coughing and spitting at police and gardaí and this might happen in certain premises, possibly where alcohol is involved.

Staff might need to have additional training in conflict management and resolution to deal with such situations. This may not be necessary in pubs and similar establishments that already employ "door staff" but could be a real need in other food premises.

No matter how many procedures are put in place and no matter how much training is given, some staff may not feel comfortable or safe working in the food business.

Covid-19 could have several implications for employer and employee relations which is well outside the scope of this book.

There are perhaps two issues that are becoming very important in the debate about re-opening the economy and the safety of people; physical distancing and the use of face coverings.

The 2-metre requirement has become so ingrained in us that there is a risk that it has entered the psyche as a mandatory rule that cannot and should not be relaxed in any way at any time. This may have been the intention of governments and advisers; after all it is a simple concept with little room for doubt as to what it means and how it should be implemented.

However, with time, businesses and business representatives have questioned the impact of 2 metre distancing on commercial viability.

Rather than it being an unbreakable, unshakeable distance, the Irish Chief Medical Officer, Dr Tony Holohan, is reported to have said that the reference to staying apart by 2 metres;

> "… is not a rule, it is guidance. It has been described as if it is some hard and fast law that is there. So it is guidance and like any guidance it has to be interpreted by people at an individual level and then by organisations."

Similar statements have been made in the UK and both jurisdictions are looking to reduce the distance, at least as it applies in some sectors, particularly hospitality.

It must be right to have the debate. However, consumers must be weaned off the expectation that 2 metres is a mandatory requirement and is the only safe distance. Businesses must demonstrate that they have taken all necessary measures to keep consumers safe at a 1 metre distance.

However, if it is shown that 1 metre, even with the additional safety measures in place, is not a safe distance then we risk going back to square one and a return to restrictions which is not in anyone's interests.

This places an even greater emphasis on appropriate and site-specific risk assessments and the implementation of proper procedures.

The 2 metre versus 1 metre debate might have been resolved by the time the book is published. However, that does not end the discussion on the measures necessary to keep staff and customers safe.

The second issue where advice and guidance has also been somewhat inconsistent and confusing is the wearing of face masks or face coverings in public.

In the UK and Ireland, the wearing of face coverings in some public settings such as in shops and on public transport has been strongly advised. This is not necessarily to protect the wearer but to protect against inadvertent transmission of the virus by people who are not showing symptoms of Covid-19.

In England, from Monday 15th June 2020, it became mandatory in England to wear a face covering on public transport including trains, buses, trams, ferries and planes and when visiting hospitals.

That requirement does not extend to Wales, Northern Ireland or to Scotland, although each justification is keeping this issue under review.

In Ireland the guidance on wearing face coverings has become much stricter in that people are being told that they should be worn in shops and on public transport.

Will the places where face coverings should be worn be extended and what implications might this have for the food industry?

As time goes on, we will need to see to what extent guidance on physical distancing and face coverings becomes translated into law, with potential fines for non-compliance.

There will be many more twists and turns before there is any semblance of continuity and consistency in the advice, guidance and law relating to Covid-19. This means that food businesses will need to keep on top of developments to see how changes affect their businesses and respond accordingly.

With a bit of planning and thought, it is probably quite easy for us, as individuals, to adhere to the guidance around physical distancing, wearing face coverings and hand hygiene.

However, this poses significant challenges for the food industry and careful, proactive and effective measures need to be taken to prevent, or at least minimise as far as possible, the spread of Covid-19. If this is not done properly, the move out of lockdown will be delayed, to the detriment of businesses, consumers and the economy.

CHAPTER TWELVE
CONCLUSION

There is no firm conclusion to the story of Covid-19 and the law relating to food.

We are certainly in the very early stages of finding a way to protect consumers while allowing businesses to open, survive and hopefully thrive.

This is essential for the health and wealth of individuals, industries and nations.

The food philosophy is determined by the owners and operators of the business, its implementation is carried out by members of staff across all areas of the operation. Everyone must work together for the common good.

Introducing measures to make premises Covid-secure while maintaining full compliance with food law and all other obligations requires a significant investment of time, thought, money and effort. This is necessary; it is not an optional extra.

Covid-19 is a very serious issue and a major threat to consumers and food businesses. By taking a step back and considering first principles about the identification of hazards and assessment of risks, it is possible to avoid becoming overwhelmed by the enormity of the situation.

Ultimately, adapting to Covid-19 is about changing perceptions, attitudes and behaviour.

Brexit, which was never out of the headlines is starting to move back into the spotlight. The current indications are that the UK will not seek an extension beyond 2020 and this might have significant consequences for a food industry that will still be fighting its way back from the impact of Covid-19.

Covid-19 has presented us with the unthinkable. People have been unable to travel freely, meet family and friends, be present with loved ones during celebrations, achievements, birth and death. The long-term personal, and therefore societal, consequences of these restrictions will be many and varied. Add these to the potential economic consequences of the virus and it can be seen that this is truly a once-in-a-lifetime experience (we hope!).

It ought to be recorded for posterity that the response to Covid-19 in Ireland was managed without a formal government being in place.

We will get through this but the impact on how we make, distribute, supply and consume food may have changed forever.

We must identify and use the positive lessons from the global, national and individual responses to Covid-19, otherwise it could be the loss of a very significant opportunity to help protect, promote and enhance food safety, food security and food sustainability.

Only time will tell if we have managed to do this.

MORE BOOKS BY LAW BRIEF PUBLISHING

A selection of our other titles available now:-

'A Practical Guide to the General Data Protection Regulation (GDPR) – 2nd Edition' by Keith Markham
'Ellis on Credit Hire – Sixth Edition' by Aidan Ellis & Tim Kevan
'A Practical Guide to Working with Litigants in Person and McKenzie Friends in Family Cases' by Stuart Barlow
'Protecting Unregistered Brands: A Practical Guide to the Law of Passing Off' by Lorna Brazell
'A Practical Guide to Secondary Liability and Joint Enterprise Post-Jogee' by Joanne Cecil & James Mehigan
'A Practical Guide to the Pre-Action RTA Claims Protocol for Personal Injury Lawyers' by Antonia Ford
'A Practical Guide to Neighbour Disputes and the Law' by Alexander Walsh
'A Practical Guide to Forfeiture of Leases' by Mark Shelton
'A Practical Guide to Coercive Control for Legal Practitioners and Victims' by Rachel Horman
'A Practical Guide to Rights Over Airspace and Subsoil' by Daniel Gatty
'Tackling Disclosure in the Criminal Courts – A Practitioner's Guide' by Narita Bahra QC & Don Ramble
'A Practical Guide to the Law of Driverless Cars – Second Edition' by Alex Glassbrook, Emma Northey & Scarlett Milligan
'A Practical Guide to TOLATA Claims' by Greg Williams
'Artificial Intelligence – The Practical Legal Issues' by John Buyers
'A Practical Guide to the Law of Prescription in Scotland' by Andrew Foyle
'A Practical Guide to the Construction and Rectification of Wills and Trust Instruments' by Edward Hewitt
'A Practical Guide to the Law of Bullying and Harassment in the Workplace' by Philip Hyland

'How to Be a Freelance Solicitor: A Practical Guide to the SRA-Regulated Freelance Solicitor Model' by Paul Bennett
'A Practical Guide to Prison Injury Claims' by Malcolm Johnson
'A Practical Guide to the Small Claims Track' by Dominic Bright
'A Practical Guide to Advising Clients at the Police Station' by Colin Stephen McKeown-Beaumont
'A Practical Guide to Antisocial Behaviour Injunctions' by Iain Wightwick
'Practical Mediation: A Guide for Mediators, Advocates, Advisers, Lawyers, and Students in Civil, Commercial, Business, Property, Workplace, and Employment Cases' by Jonathan Dingle with John Sephton
'The Mini-Pupillage Workbook' by David Boyle
'A Practical Guide to Crofting Law' by Brian Inkster
'A Practical Guide to Spousal Maintenance' by Liz Cowell
'A Practical Guide to the Law of Domain Names and Cybersquatting' by Andrew Clemson
'A Practical Guide to the Law of Gender Pay Gap Reporting' by Harini Iyengar
'A Practical Guide to the Rights of Grandparents in Children Proceedings' by Stuart Barlow
'NHS Whistleblowing and the Law' by Joseph England
'Employment Law and the Gig Economy' by Nigel Mackay & Annie Powell
'A Practical Guide to Noise Induced Hearing Loss (NIHL) Claims' by Andrew Mckie, Ian Skeate, Gareth McAloon
'An Introduction to Beauty Negligence Claims – A Practical Guide for the Personal Injury Practitioner' by Greg Almond
'Intercompany Agreements for Transfer Pricing Compliance' by Paul Sutton
'Zen and the Art of Mediation' by Martin Plowman
'A Practical Guide to the SRA Principles, Individual and Law Firm Codes of Conduct 2019 – What Every Law Firm Needs to Know' by Paul Bennett
'A Practical Guide to Adoption for Family Lawyers' by Graham Pegg
'A Practical Guide to Industrial Disease Claims' by Andrew Mckie & Ian Skeate
'A Practical Guide to Redundancy' by Philip Hyland
'A Practical Guide to Vicarious Liability' by Mariel Irvine

'A Practical Guide to Applications for Landlord's Consent and Variation of Leases' by Mark Shelton
'A Practical Guide to Relief from Sanctions Post-Mitchell and Denton' by Peter Causton
'A Practical Guide to Equity Release for Advisors' by Paul Sams
'A Practical Guide to Unlawful Eviction and Harassment' by Stephanie Lovegrove
'A Practical Guide to the Law Relating to Food' by Ian Thomas
'A Practical Guide to Financial Services Claims' by Chris Hegarty
'The Law of Houses in Multiple Occupation: A Practical Guide to HMO Proceedings' by Julian Hunt
'A Practical Guide to Unlawful Eviction and Harassment' by Stephanie Lovegrove
'A Practical Guide to Solicitor and Client Costs' by Robin Dunne
'Occupiers, Highways and Defective Premises Claims: A Practical Guide Post-Jackson – 2nd Edition' by Andrew Mckie
'A Practical Guide to Financial Ombudsman Service Claims' by Adam Temple & Robert Scrivenor
'A Practical Guide to the Law of Enfranchisement and Lease Extension' by Paul Sams
'A Practical Guide to Marketing for Lawyers – 2nd Edition' by Catherine Bailey & Jennet Ingram
'A Practical Guide to Advising Schools on Employment Law' by Jonathan Holden
'A Practical Guide to Running Housing Disrepair and Cavity Wall Claims: 2nd Edition' by Andrew Mckie & Ian Skeate
'A Practical Guide to Holiday Sickness Claims – 2nd Edition' by Andrew Mckie & Ian Skeate
'Arguments and Tactics for Personal Injury and Clinical Negligence Claims' by Dorian Williams
'A Practical Guide to QOCS and Fundamental Dishonesty' by James Bentley
'A Practical Guide to Drone Law' by Rufus Ballaster, Andrew Firman, Eleanor Clot
'A Practical Guide to Compliance for Personal Injury Firms Working With Claims Management Companies' by Paul Bennett
'A Practical Guide to the Landlord and Tenant Act 1954: Commercial Tenancies' by Richard Hayes & David Sawtell

'A Practical Guide to Dog Law for Owners and Others' by Andrea Pitt
'RTA Allegations of Fraud in a Post-Jackson Era: The Handbook – 2nd Edition' by Andrew Mckie
'RTA Personal Injury Claims: A Practical Guide Post-Jackson' by Andrew Mckie
'On Experts: CPR35 for Lawyers and Experts' by David Boyle
'An Introduction to Personal Injury Law' by David Boyle
'A Practical Guide to Claims Arising From Accidents Abroad and Travel Claims' by Andrew Mckie & Ian Skeate
'A Practical Guide to Chronic Pain Claims' by Pankaj Madan
'A Practical Guide to Claims Arising from Fatal Accidents' by James Patience
'A Practical Approach to Clinical Negligence Post-Jackson' by Geoffrey Simpson-Scott
'Employers' Liability Claims: A Practical Guide Post-Jackson' by Andrew Mckie
'A Practical Guide to Subtle Brain Injury Claims' by Pankaj Madan
'A Practical Guide to Costs in Personal Injury Cases' by Matthew Hoe
'The No Nonsense Solicitors' Practice: A Guide To Running Your Firm' by Bettina Brueggemann
'The Queen's Counsel Lawyer's Omnibus: 20 Years of Cartoons from The Times 1993-2013' by Alex Steuart Williams

www.ingramcontent.com/pod-product-compliance
Ingram Content Group UK Ltd.
Pitfield, Milton Keynes, MK11 3LW, UK
UKHW020149290926
15471UKWH00004B/774

9 781913 715038